Areej, who is still waiting for her 12th birthday, had started penning down her thoughts and emotions as poems when she was nine. Areej has gone through a rollercoaster of emotions and those up and downs of her life can be seen in her poems. Areej left behind the luxuries and friends she grew up with in U.A.E., as her father lost his job, which led to her moving to India. There, she realized the true meaning of struggle without her protective father. Bouncing back to U.A.E. after two years, Areej found a better version of herself.

For my beloved sister, Selina Khan, who is an outspoken critic and silent admirer of my work and my incredible and inspirational parents, M. Shafquat Khan and Heena Kausar.

With love,
AK

Areej Khan

WHO RULES THE WORLD IN WONDERLAND?

AUSTIN MACAULEY PUBLISHERS™

LONDON • CAMBRIDGE • NEW YORK • SHARJAH

ISBN – 9789948797517– (Paperback)
ISBN – 9789948797524– (E-Book)

Application Number: MC-10-01-9376782
Age Classification: E

Printer Name: iPrint Global Ltd
Printer Address: Witchford, England

First Published 2023
AUSTIN MACAULEY PUBLISHERS FZE
Sharjah Publishing City
P.O Box [519201]
Sharjah, UAE
www.austinmacauley.ae
+971 655 95 202

I'm greatly thankful to my publishers for recognizing my work, making it immortal to the world, and keeping faith on an unknown poet. These publishers are high-minded and extremely generous people.

The rest of my gratitude is due in four quarters.

Firstly, my mother, Heena Kausar, who inspired many of my decisions in life, including this part. She helped me name some of my poems, and has always encouraged me to follow my dreams. I thank God for making her my mother, as I cannot imagine life without her.

Secondly, my father, Mohammad Shafquat Khan, who has also helped me in various faces of my life, and faced problems upfront, even in the roughest years. I thank him for being so brave and inspiring, to the point he never let the bitter taste of life seep into mine.

Thirdly, my sister, Selina Khan, who was a major inspiration for my poems. A sweet memory I have is when I wrote my first poem for her on her birthday a few years back. She has been a constant inspiration for so many of my poems, I have lost count. I thank her for being so trustworthy, it made her the best companion of life I had so far.

Lastly, my English teacher, whose teaching skills of English as a subject improved my language as well as helped me regain my lost interest in literature. I thank her for being so kind a teacher.

Apart from them, I thank all my friends and extended family for always being there for me.

Table of Contents

Preface   **13**

Jubilance   **17**

   Paint   19

   Stars   20

   Friendship   21

   A Night in June   23

   Rainforests   24

   Hobbyhorse   25

   Philosopher's Day   26

Vendetta   **29**

   Wisteria (Pt.1)   31

   Mad Woman   32

   My Vengeance   34

   Wisteria (Pt.2)   36

   The Advice / Mom   37

Turmoil   **39**

   What's Next?   41

   Did You?   42

Surveillance Surfs 43

No 45

Stroke of Luck 46

Light 47

Make Me Want You 48

Agony **53**

Undesirable Existence 55

Wishes 56

Scars 58

Core 59

Eraser 60

Sheepdog 61

Dig, Digger 62

Time 64

Don't Paint Me the Bad Guy 65

Clownery **69**

The Fungi 71

Humans? 72

Mouthful 73

18 Century 74

Exploratory **77**

Masquerade 79

World Wide Web 80

Differences   81

Reality   82

Truce   83

Sweet and Sour   84

Magical Writing   85

Preface

I've spent the last two years making memories and penning it down onto diaries and into poems. In this collection of poems I've selected, you'll practically see me in my truest form of the time. I've penned down my feelings on diaries but none of it ever felt as mystical as creating poems. Throughout the collection of poems, you will see me as where I was at the time of life I penned down the poem.

I remember thinking like a storyteller at some point, few weeks or months later being so vulnerable, then joking around like a jokester. Sometimes, during the penning down of the poems, I felt free and at top of the world, like I was at the peak of my youth. Other times, I felt lost, confused, sad, misunderstood, and felt like I could run to the top of a cliff and just yell all my frustrations away.

The gift of storytelling is something I will forever cherish. It feels so natural writing and reading poems, being able to create characters, tell their stories, all in a few lines. Throughout my school years, I've read poems and stories but for me, I've never actually understood what those stories are trying to convey. Instead, I've fallen in love with the magic and mystery of poetry.

So, in conclusion, I hope you enjoy poems depicting my life in the past two years. Solid poems of vulnerability, happiness, sadness, storytelling, humor, etc. Practically me trying to find myself while holding onto the thin thread keeping me sane, down to earth, and keeping me from losing love; the thread which is so close to breaking. Enjoy!!!

Jubilance

Paint

The paint that sprays my veins,
Is something that could change my mood today.
I was filled with angst,
But as soon as I saw the paint,
My mood changed in its grace.

They come in many colors,
Pink, green, jade, and red.
Oh! Those lovely colors could paint the sky the darkest gray.
They paint me blue.
Blue. Lost in mist.

It's calming.
It's soothing.
It's free.
And that's what makes it so much more
Special to me.

Stars

Far, far away,
Maybe in space.
Lay a little creature
Who didn't know its place.

It was bright,
It shone light.
Like a heavenly creature.

For me and my friend
Find and see it every night.

It is just a misplaced star,
Pretending to shine
With all its might.
In a foreign solar system
That knows its line.

Friendship

My friendship with my best friend
Is something I would never forget.

From her loyalty, honesty, and generosity
Which honestly melts my heart in two.
Some qualities that I could never forge,
For the sake of our friendship,
I'll hold you on those horrid days.

Never going to be the same
If you were to leave me.
Keep me company every night and day,
And give me all of you.

I hope I don't ask for much
Because you've already given a lot.
I will give you the same
With no disdain.
Be with you through hard and soft,
With no doubt that you'll change the way
Of the world,
And its rage.
Don't change, oh please don't!
You're the best and
I love you so much.

What's my hand
Without your heart to hold.
I'll be with you,
Even when the spirit leaves the bone.

I will be with you through all,
Even when your heart breaks.
I'll be there to wipe your tears,
And tuck your hair behind your ears.
Until you're at rest.

We will be together,
Till death do us part,
Or maybe never…

Our friendship is one to treasure,
Don't forget about us.
Don't forget the memories you made with me.

Hope you'll never regret holding my hand,
From primary to forever after.

Be proud of your will,
I know you will change the world.

A Night in June

A beautiful night in June
Is what I recall
From last night.

Late night walks,
The summer lighting in summer times.

Beauty for one
Is found
Not in body
Or looks
But in souls and my city.

Oh, what a wonderful place to live,
This is what I recall
From last night in June.

Rainforests

The ethereal feelings I feel,
As I walk through the rainforest,
Are as peaceful as the sky
On a day with good weather.

The euphoria is as exiting
As the serenity and peace
That fulfils each and every
Breath I take.

The way the water runs
On every cliff it passes
Is as nerve-racking as it is beautiful.

The aroma of aromatic trees
Is what attracts me
To the amazing rainforest.

Hobbyhorse

My hobby is very different,
It's very hard to perfect.
But once you get the hang of it,
It's very hard to forget.

You should never swim in the cold,
It will make you very bold.
Swimming is my vent,
That made it to the Olympic events.

Philosopher's Day

"Welcome! Welcome!" she said that day,
"Smile! Smile!" she said with faith.
Sadness and cries
Can be fixed
With one of her smiles.

With eyes that sparkle in the night,
A will to meet us every day,
That we can say the same.

She is the teacher of this class,
Not any class,
Her class.

Come and smile for a moment,
And scream "Happy Teachers Day!"
When she walks in that day.

A beautiful time.
It's time to see all teachers smile!

Vendetta

Wisteria (Pt.1)

Isn't it mysterious?
How I look myself in the mirror and
Smile to something you'll never know?

How you think that just because
I'm friendly with people,
They're my friends?
They're not.

Isn't it mysterious,
When I appreciate someone
Through my elegies,
You'll probably never know who
It's about?

Isn't it mysterious?

Mad Woman

Out of her best albums
She wrote was poetry.

Good to bad
Occurs quickly.
When men lie
Under your nose.

A story they hid so well,
To wish they didn't
Read those.

"There is nothing without trust,"
He said as he broke the same trust
You gave him.

Something he realized
After the color
From your face
Drains.

Sick of their lies,
Sick of their games.
You decide as you walk out
With rage.

"Bye-bye," you say
To that Pink city
You and him built with lies.

As you plan your revenge,
You find your light
In that mad woman
That saved your life.

My Vengeance

We listen to an artist
Who is known for wise words.

Surprised with her poetry,
We laughed in spite of knowing.

Those movies we saw,
We laughed at, became real
As I realized the sin
You committed.

You read my diaries,
Knowing what you hid…
Your wish to not have read those
Increase as you see me fill with rage.

I walk out,
Knowing that I will get my revenge…
You burned the roses and cities we built.
No laws gave misfortune liberation.

Me who could not have
Lived in that city
Said "Good day, buddy"
In that place you said was safe.

I run into the woman
You hate with your life.

Wisteria (Pt.2)

You want to unravel my mysteries,
But you're consumed in someone
I call my best friend.

She was the kindest woman I knew,
So, I fight the urge.
Little did I realize,
He was soon to bicker.

She was mad.
We knew the contents,
And words which filled her diaries.
Only to break her trust.

Just for the suspense.
The scene is imprinted in my mind,
She walks out in rage.
I don't know where she went,
But by the looks of it,
He's got the rest figured.

Knowing the sin,
All I saw was dim.
He too saw no luck in finding her.

The Advice / Mom

She came,
I heard her rush through my door,
To see shock.

She cried and rampaged
On and on
About them.

I was mad.
But I took my anger
And made a mastermind
Of a plan.

Realizing they got married
In the fun of the greenery.
In the magic of time,
This made the plan better.

Turmoil

What's Next?

I feel scared,
Scared of the haunts in my head,
Scared of the voices in my head.

What's next?

When I look into the mirror,
I don't see a beautiful future.
I see one of success,
But with a room of sorrow.

But the lingering question still haunts,
…what's next?
Greedy of me think I have another day to live.
Today, I will determine what to do as of every second,
And let the future unfold,
And hold it in hands,
Willing to stitch it into
A happy, successful, and safe future.
That's what's next.

Did You?

Did you do what you weren't to do at fifteen?
Or at the age of fifteen,
Did you do something that you shouldn't have?

At twenty-two,
Did you achieve everything you wanted?
Or did you achieve
Everything you wanted at twenty-two?

Did you reach your goals at thirty-one?
Or at thirty-one, did you reach your goals
Which seemed to be far away?

Surveillance Surfs

When I fell,
I fell apart.
Stretched my muscles on the ground,
I once decorated
Like a kid with colored markers.

When I rose,
I heard screams
Of help, sorrow, and sadness.

Then I heard a yell,
That I wasn't many,
That I wasn't many reasons to be loved for.
Then I heard a holler
Of worry.
She told me to hurry.
I hid under the bed.
I heard glass breaking before…
Murder.
My mom, my cat, and her.
The most special.

He sat on the couch.
The nerve. The audacity.
The aura he shed off,

One that one could easily be mistaken for a kind soul.
I was angry.
Went to kitchen,
Picked up a knife and a pan.
Hit him with both in my hands.

Late was I to realize the crime I did.
The way I was no different than him.

Always, I was told,
That there were monsters under my bed.
That when I didn't surrender to sleep,
They were to haunt me, forevermore.

If they were to get to me
The legal authorities,
What would become of me?

I hid under the bed.
Quick was I to realize
There was none of such monsters described to me.
It then occurred to me,
I was the monster.

Now what?
Every night in the surveillance of the midnight moon,
Every kid wonders,
"When we fall into slumber, who rules the wonder?"

No

No, I never said that.
I promise, I never did.
Only those believe that,
Those who ever did.

The pleads echo,
Down the empty halls.
For whom
To hear?

He's caught on camera.
There's no escape.
No way
To ignore the punishment.

His "Nos"
Couldn't be
Any less significant.

Stroke of Luck

If everyone could,
Everyone would
Count all misfortune,
Then deem themselves
As someone who calls upon bad.

But if everyone could,
No one would
Count all good.
Then deem themselves
As someone who calls upon good.

If they did,
Where would all the children go?

Light

Left you in the morning light,
Saw you at midnight.
Loved at sunrise.
Fell out at sunset.

My Sagittarius
Making its presence known.
My mastery in dishonesty.
Your loss at the game
Of life and manipulation.

All at the blessing
And curse
Of the light
Shone by the sun
Itself and the moon included.

Make Me Want You

The last time you ever did something nice
Was when I saw you.
And you saw me.

It was a nice moment,
It was a rekindling moment
When I met you again
A few days ago.

I thought you deserved more,
So I gave you more.
You threw it in the dustbin,
Like it was nothing.
But deep down,
I knew it was something.

You broke me,
Into ten million pieces,
But it's all okay now.
I've learned to be satisfied,
With my worn-out self.

Now it is the end,
And you want to start again,
But all I have to say is,

"Make me want you"
Or else, leave.

The door isn't far out,
And you have legs,
So leave.
Just leave.

I don't love you anymore,
Why can't you see?

It's the end for us,
Its halfway out the door for you.
If what I ever wanted
Never mattered to you,
Why should yours matter
To me?

I was foolish,
But now I've learned.
If I want love,
It means,
I want power.

Your story is only half-written
And whenever I tried
To write your book,
You took the quill away from me.
Now, you are willing to give back the quill,
But I am waiting for you
To take it back.

My respect,
My love.
My trust.
My poems.
My stories.

Was my love,
All pigeon-like to you?
Come and leave,
Whenever you liked?
Or found comfortable?

If so,
"Make me want you"
So, I don't have to worry
About you leaving
Anymore.

I don't love you anymore,
But I know somebody else will.
Stop wasting your precious time on me.
Find that person.

For when you'd leave all
Your bare necessities
That someone who's
Willing to want you,
Because that person is not me.
My person will be here soon,
So leave.
I want you on the other side of the door.

It's all so sickening to watch,
If you are not able to leave,
You give me no choice
But to kick you out.

Make her want you,
So, it won't end up
Like us.

Agony

Undesirable Existence

I woke in joy.
Knew nothing of sorrow.
Ran to the kitchen, for water.
At last, after an eight-hour round,
None of water, just sleep and incredible madness.

Ma told me there was no water, no tea.
Went to the well,
Then saw a grampus
Lying near the sea.

Then I finally understood
The sorrow it had seen.
Checked under the blanket
Of the white-blue sea.

Saw plastic under
That I've seen before.
But how quick I was to almost ignore
The sorrow of animals
Under the now blue-black sea.

All I'd call
An undesirable existence.

Wishes

One wish,
Just because you're hurt.
One wish,
For another one.
One wish,
For me.

No greed.
No bill.
Just because I'm hurt.
No 'we',
No 'will'.
They say, one wish will fix another one.

When you're hurt, you survive,
But when she's hurt…
Will I cry?
I want to cry.
I really do.

I seem more hurt
Because of you.
Why?
Because I love you.

I want to take the pain away,
I wish I could.
Why?
You seem to not have been bothered
Because of this.
Every morning, I wake up,
In bed
Next to you.

Every time you move twice,
My heart stammers,
On its way to its next beat.

If you're hurt or not,
I have one wish,
For you to know, I love you.

Scars

Mental, physical, and emotional
Are all made to go
One day,
Not now.

One day,
Probably at the end of the world,
The sears will be nowhere
Near fatal.

I promise they'll heal,
Even if at the moment,
The promise seems empty
And hard to believe.

At the end of day,
You will feel better
Than the morning.
So, for the day to end
Peacefully.

Core

Her core is very special,
Every time,
Between now and then,
Her hands shake
Uncontrollably.

I wonder why.
I love her a lot.
Why she was chosen to struggle?
I wish I could take the pain away.

After all,
I don't want to break her core.

Eraser

I wish I could erase my past mistakes,
So I would not be one of many
To get a glimpse
Of Sadness, misery, and misfortune.

I am not a wisher.
Wishing on wishing
Will not give me an eraser.

Something that could erase
My past mistakes,
Would always make me
A sinner.

Sheepdog

Am I a sheepdog to you?
Do I round up the sheep for you?
Do I do it perfectly
Enough for you?

Do you know
How much it hurts?
How much it destroys my ego?
How you lessen so much
Of my self-respect?
How much it hurt me?

I'll never be good enough for you.
I hope you'll never know
The feeling of being
In the darkest room of life.

Dig, Digger

Dig me a hole
Deep enough to lay my body.

So deep,
That no one can hear me
When I change my mind.

But before I go,
Take me to the top of the world.
I want to look at the world
Before I leave.
I want to taste the salt in my tears
And the metals in my blood.

Paint me gold
And blue
Before I leave.
So, dig, digger.

Quick.
Before they see.

Tell my friends,
I hate them.
Tell my family,

I will always love, appreciate, and cherish them.
Good bye.

Time

Time is special,
Time is precious.
It's more words could ever be.

I've learned to be sinister,
For everything I do,
A critic awaits.
Coming from him it seems
Oh, so disgusting.

If time is money,
He's bankrupt.
He had the gun,
I gave the bullets.

And now I have to pay.
I hope he sees this.

Don't Paint Me the Bad Guy

I was not in the good
When you left.

I was still a small-town girl,
Known to no one.

I never wanted your drama.
You came to me.

You paint me a portrait of me,
But all I can see,
How you paint me the bad guy.

It was your choice to dance
In my storm.

It was perfect,
Until you made it all wrong.

Not once,
Not twice,
Not even three times.

Had you ever told me
You were leaving?

After a good weekend,
Are you sure you don't feel anything?
I felt something.
Deeper than a weekend.
Deeper than the sweat.

All the sweat I put in "us,"
If only it were just a weekend.

Did you not feel anything?

Was that why you painted me
The bad guy?

Was it so easy for you
To make me the bad guy?
That easy?

When I left,
Did it feel right?

When I was right,
Did you feel heart-broken?

Don't make me the bad guy
When it was as much your fault
As it was mine.

Clownery

The Fungi

What if fungi had a heart?
Would it still send yeast on my bread?
What if fungi had a heart?
Would its mushrooms still grow
Over those beautiful trees?

What a mysterious question,
So surreal…
But a good query.
Sometimes, like a deal.

What if fungi had a heart?
Would it have a weakness?

Humans?

What if humans had green pigment?
Would they turn green?
What if humans were green?
Would we change our niceties?

A question with no answer,
Scientists try but fail.
The politicians—
The same.

What if humans had green pigment?
Would they have veins?

Mouthful

A fist-full of chips,
In my mouth they go.
They will never return,
That I know.

Then my mom walks in,
In goes the food,
In one gulp.
She becomes mad,
And gives me a mouthful.

18 Century

Welcome to the 18 century,
There's a lot to say.
You either will be loved,
Or be deemed a disgrace.

To the men that know you,
And others that don't,
All you will ever be in their eyes
Is a person of the syndicate.

Welcome to the 18 century,
There's a lot to say.
It's easier to get famous,
But the critics will replace

All the self-confidence
With a really easy blow.
Because in the end,
All you ever were,
Were a girl.

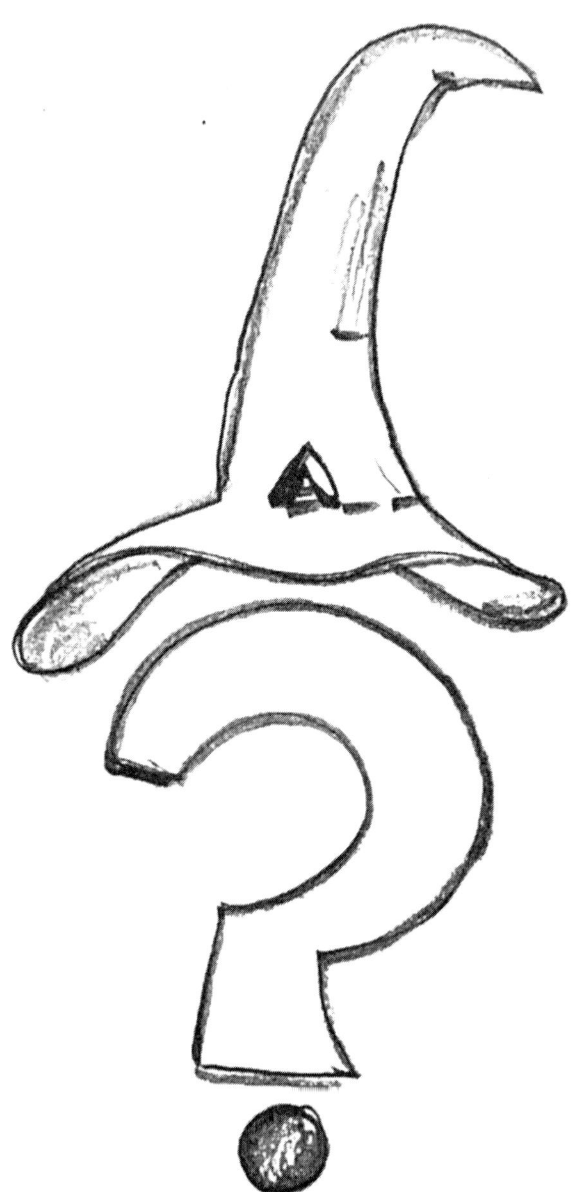

Exploratory

Masquerade

People amid circumstances
Met some people after lockdown.
People in and people out.

Got some things,
Get some out.
People in and people out.

Got some tea
On all the crisscrossed fortune tellers,
Haven't felt it in a while.

So who am I to say?
I'm a person too,
Just in a mask,
Walking in a masquerade.

World Wide Web

Net's a weird place,
I thought that Internet was so untrustworthy,
My Snapchat location is always off.
My Instagram posts

Limited to only three.
Net's such a weird place,
I met some good people here too!
No wait, I take it back.

How dare you lose my trust?
And how dare you fuel more issues
In trust?
It's a game of lost and found,
I lost before I could even find you.

Net is such a weird place,
Never thought I'd learn so much
At a young age,
So much about life.

Differences

Everyone is different,
And have a different story to tell.
Everyone is unique,
Peach, brown, black, and white
From the eyes to the toes,

Green, orange, brown, black, and blue.
To be similar,
We have to be different.
Let's see who can blame you.
Be yourself,
Because the idols
Who you look up to
Were different to be
Your idol.

Reality

When the moon sets
And the eyes get wet
Of the sun rising,
When Luna sets.

The eyes unfold,
The lies get told.
The buses move as
The brushes move.

Something different every day.
After the moon sets,
And the sun lets,
Light shines
On our holy faces
As we lie.

Let not the past define you,
Because your past isn't you.
People don't define you,
Even though they lie to you.
You are different.
The reality is different.
Be different.

Truce

Compared to the history of its ancestors
The past lived in peace, tolerance, and honesty.
But now I suffocate
At the smell of the world's dishonesty.

What a corrupted world,
Thinking that they're right.
Fooling themselves into believing
That they live in peace.

If there was one wish
God could grant,
It would be to remind the people of the world
Of their morals.

As peaceful as the blue sky.
For the world to live in harmony,
There is a long way to go.
Amen.

Sweet and Sour

Honey is sweet,
Milk is sour.
My lovely food necessities
Matches my daily needs.

You be the honey.
I'll be the milk.
We'll be together forever after.
All you have to say is
'Yes.'

No.
Never.
I wasn't made to be lovesick.
I was made to be the chaser.
It's who I am.

Milk and honey
Sweet, right?

Magical Writing

Arts and pictures
Through the text
Can only support
All of what left.

Pick up a quill
And write your heart out
Till there is no ink
Left in the inkpot.

Do not commit.
Shift genres.
Styles and questions.
"What is all this sweet work worth,
If you not love me?"

Make scenarios,
Imaginary or real.
Once again,
Do not commit!

Lies and lines.
Pictures and textures.
Combine to form a bit
Of poetry.

Not easy, I know.
But just pick up a quill and follow
All your heart's desires
Left in the back of the cupboard.

Open and set free in your own
Little world.
Nothing worth
To pond over
Time long past.

This magical writing
Can only support
What's in your mind,
Don't have to even say a word.

Books and books,
Till you're left
Bare. In hindsight.

Leave. Now.
There is no turning back now.
Pick up the typewriter
And write
Your heart out.

Feel and write,
What you feel is right
To you,
In this present time.